It's Not About
The Game

It's Not About The Game

Kevin Siedlecki

Great Point Publishing, LLC

Gloversville, NY

It's Not About The Game
Kevin Siedlecki

Cover Design By: Great Point Publishing LLC
Book design by: Great Point Publishing LLC

To order additional copies of this title, contact your favorite local bookstore or visit *www.greatpointpublishing.com*

Paperback ISBN: 978-1-955334-35-8
Hardcover ISBN: 978-1-955334-34-1

Printed in the United States of America

Published by: **Great Point Publishing, LLC.**
Gloversville, NY

Dedication.

To Dad- For showing me how to be a coach and a man.

To Mom- For supporting everything I ever tried, and the wisdom that "the team does not belong to the coach."

Cheers and Applause for It's Not About The Game...

"There are so many great life lessons in this book. If you are a coach or an athletic director, you need to add this to your library."

>   *-Jake von Scherrer*
>   *Host of The Educational AD Podcast*
>   *Tavares, FL*

"Kevin is a transformational leader. His message to coaches and athletes reminds me of greats like John Wooden and Steve Kerr."

>   *-Craig Semple*
>   *Former Athletics Director*
>   *Daniel Hand High School*
>   *Madison, CT*

"As a hockey player there are many aspects of this book that can be applied throughout all sports. The quote 'what you communicate to your players matters and creates a culture of deliberate behavior, not just rule following' is something I think all coaches need to see and follow with their players."

>   *- Colton Bobowski*
>   *Clinton Senior High School*
>   *Clinton, NY*

Table of Contents

It's Not About The Game

Foreword

"It's Not About the Game" explores the impact of coaching on athletes, offering insights and personal experiences to help guide future coaches in creating a successful program. Kevin Siedlecki offers a perspective of coaching that doesn't just focus on wins and losses, but rather on developing athletes into successful adults outside of sports. With years of experience, Siedlecki shares stories from practices, one-on-one conversations, and difficult coaching decisions to reveal a deeper meaning of coaching. With a blend of hard-earned wisdom, common cliches and practical advice, this book challenges coaches to look past performance stats and invest in the personal growth of individual athletes–helping them build confidence, develop a strong work ethic, and learn important life skills that will help them in their future endeavors.

This book is more than just a guidebook on how to coach, but rather a message for coaches who want to make a meaningful impact on their players. By focusing on mentorship and genuine engagement, Siedlecki reveals how fostering a culture of personal accountability leads to both team and individual success on and off the field. This book serves as a powerful reminder that the true measure of a coach's success isn't found in the trophy case, but rather the people their athletes become outside of their sport.

-Nolan Tutty
April 10, 2025
Ilion, NY

It's Not About The Mistakes

In today's culture, we don't like to forgive people. One mistake is grounds for being "canceled," fired, and ostracized. This is especially true for high school and youth coaches. Our mistakes can have a tremendous negative impact on the lives of those in our charge. What we risk forgetting as coaches is that we have as many years as we want and potentially hundreds of athletes to coach. In contrast, each individual athlete only gets to play high school sports once. We can be 99% perfect, but when we mess up 1% of the time, and that mistake affects a student-athlete, that is 100% of *their* experience. When the coach's mistake has a negative impact on them, that is their only experience with the coach and with the sport. So they have a right to be upset, and so do their parents. The parents are just tapping into their loving urge to protect and promote their children. Unfortunately, too often, neither parents nor administrators are satisfied with a coach apologizing and learning. Coaches are expected to be perfect at all times.

Like anyone else, I am not a perfect coach. However, I have been incredibly lucky to have athletic directors who understand this. The first, Craig Semple, hired me when I was a hyper-competitive (read: cocky) 26-year-old with limited experience as an assistant coach, but he believed I could grow to be a great coach, and he let me grow. When he saw or heard of me being less than perfect, he didn't run scared of parents. He talked to me, and he helped me grow. Without that kind of support, I never could have become a good coach. I could have been fired after a couple years, never given the opportunity to learn. Then I would have either moved on to another team, a better coach than I was before learning from that mistake, or never coached again.

This book is a result of my mistakes. I apologize to all the athletes these mistakes affected negatively. I hope that whether you are a coach or an athlete reading this, that you can learn from my mistakes instead of having to make the same type of mistakes yourself. In so many schools and towns throughout the country these days, you will not be given the opportunity to learn from your own mistakes, so I hope you can learn from mine.

That being said, I did not set out to write this book because I have some innate sense of how to coach that is better than anyone else's. I started writing as an act of reflection, to see what I could learn about myself and, in the process, to see what I could improve in my coaching practice. It didn't take me long to realize that pretty much every insight I had was due to a mistake I made. That should not have come as a surprise. I preach to my athletes that every failure is a learning opportunity, and I have often said that no one could have taught me how to teach or coach by explaining how to do it. I have been very lucky to be surrounded by athletes, parents, coaches, and administrators who have supported me through the best and lowest moments. No matter how much they work and learn, every coach needs to make his or her own mistakes. There is no teacher like failure.

This book is purposefully not a practical "how-to" of actionable steps to make yourself a better coach. What works for me won't necessarily work for you. In fact, what works for me one year with one set of athletes probably won't work for me in another year with a different group. Coaching is about constantly improving, being yourself, and maintaining your values while adapting to new athletes and teams. So this book does not offer drills and activities that will improve your team because drills and activities don't matter nearly as much as the attitude with which you present them. I cannot tell you that anything will work any particular day, but I can present the mentality that goes into building a good team. This book is about the driving principles of coaching, a step or two removed from Xs and Os or practice planning, to the rationale for those plays and plans. Why do we do what we do? I wrote this book to explore my *why* and, in the process, developed a stronger philosophy. No one can tell a coach how to coach any given team in any sport, any season, but we can start to think about what drives our decisions. I reflected on my first decade as a coach, and through the successes and failures (mostly failures) of coaching with deliberate focus on my philosophy, I sharpened that philosophy.

In short, this book is not intended to be a blueprint for you to apply to your coaching but to push you to think about what you do, how you do it, and why. For me, asking myself those questions opened up huge new possibilities that I implemented during the writing process. It doesn't really matter *what* you do. If you have a clear, well-communicated set of priorities that drive you to do it, it will work more often than not. This book is meant to help you think about those priorities.

Businessman and author Brian Will writes in his excellent book, <u>The Dropout Millionaire</u>, *"What I want you to understand is, while I failed, I also learned. That is why I love the phrase... 'Sometimes you win... sometimes you learn.'.... Failing is the key to success!"* [1]

Remember, it's not about the mistakes. No matter how much you work and learn as a coach, as an athlete, as a future coach, or in your career, there is no teacher like failure. As the cliché goes, when you fail once, fail again, but fail better. This book is about my mistakes. Now I want to help you avoid those same mistakes, I want to help you learn, and I want to help you win! Let's begin!

Chapter 1

It's Not About The Win

We play to win. We want to win. But we cannot over-emphasize winning to our athletes. Sometimes winning is out of our control, and if winning is the most important thing we can do, then athletes can give up when it looks like they won't win. "Second place is the first loser," goes the old saying, but when we think that way, we send the message that nothing is worth doing if you are not the best at it. There are all kinds of problems with that thinking, in sports and in the world outside sports. Besides, no team can go undefeated forever.

However, winning is important, and the desire to win is important, because the results of games can give us feedback on our performance and a tangible goal to which all the other lessons lead. Winning is a habit that is built through the building of other, smaller, more significant habits. As coaches, we can take advantage of our athletes' desire to win in order to teach them the lessons we want them to learn. Usually, coaches who are focused on life lessons and big-picture mentalities build a winning team: a team that remains focused and driven through highs and lows. Winning happens in a moment, but character, integrity, and values are always a work in progress.

"Winning happens in a moment, but character, integrity, and values are always a work in progress."

It's About Preparation

Because of an innate, competitive drive to win, the game gives us something to prepare for that athletes are invested in. They care about winning, so they are willing to do things they wouldn't otherwise do if they believe those things could make the difference between winning and losing. Athletes will run sprints, not because they love running or because the coach says so, but because they know running prepares them for the game. Being better conditioned means being less likely to tire at the end of the game and therefore more likely to win.

During practice, we always emphasize getting better, making each other better, and reaching new levels of skill as a team. We do not talk about what we are doing in relation to other teams, and we do not emphasize the end of season individual accolades and championships that we hope to earn. We set those goals at the beginning of the year and then forget about them until the time comes that they become immediate. Everything in between is focused on preparing for the moments those external goals can be reached.

Every really big game I have coached, my preseason message has been the same. Basically, I tell the team that they are prepared; they have been preparing since the first day they stepped on a field and started learning how to play the sport. All of the sprints, the challenges in practice, the film study, and the scouting reports have led to this game. They could not be more ready. The only thing between them and their goal now is to play a game they've been playing since they were six years old. Feeling prepared for anything allows for calm, confident performance.

At the start of my career, I emphasized winning too much. Too often, practice emphasized preparing for the next game. I created detailed scouting reports and even had our second string run the offensive and defensive looks we would see from our opponents. That's necessary in football, when play stops after seven seconds and everyone lines up again to do something very specific for the next play. But in a flow sport like lacrosse, soccer, or basketball, it is not as important. We want to prepare, but the game is too unpredictable to think that much while you're playing. Add in the factor that we play two to three games a week, instead of the one you play in football, and it doesn't take much experience to predict that giving too much information can be more dangerous than giving too little.

I eventually figured out that my athletes often entered games overwhelmed with information. They had a different game plan and a different set of things to think about each game. They played stiff, uncertain, scared. A few years into my career, some athletes mentioned that the scouting reports might not be as helpful as I thought, and an assistant coach suggested to me that maybe we did not have to know everything the opponent was doing if we were good enough to adjust to anything a team might do.

I started focusing a lot more on process, emphasizing each practice as a chance to improve as individuals and as a team. Most of every practice was spent developing individual skills and learning concepts that could be applied to a variety of opponents. Basically, I started teaching a single coherent set of skills and concepts, instead of teaching to each game as if it were almost a different sport, with different principles of play. I cut my scouting reports to half-page reminders of the basics that would be important for our success. Against a fast-paced team, the scouting report emphasized maintaining possession to slow them down. Against a good goalie, it emphasized taking only high-percentage shots. The only thing that would be very different from one game to the next would be defensive matchups, tailored to the strengths and weaknesses of our defenders and the opponent's biggest scoring threats, but it always rotated among the same few defenders. All they had to remember was the number of their girl that day. The more direct scouting report became a smaller, easier-to-digest piece of the preparation for playing every game to the best of our ability, instead of the focus of the days leading up to each game. The emphasis in messaging shifted from "Let's win the next game" to "Let's play as well as we can next game."

Of course, things will happen, in games and in life, that we cannot anticipate. If we are prepared for the things we know will happen, the one girl who rolls the crease well, the play the teams always sets when in a power play situation, whether the defense will be a man or zone, and we've worked on the fundamentals of the game enough to be confident that no matter what the opponent does, we will catch our passes, take good shots, and get most draws and ground balls. We can be flexible when the unexpected happens. That is a lesson that matters. Win or lose, if you've prepared the best you can, the rest is not always in your control. Beyond sports, the lesson obviously holds true. You might not know exactly what will happen in a job interview, a performance review, or a sales pitch, but if you've prepared for the kinds of questions you know are likely to be asked, if you've practiced your intonation, studied your material, then much of that professional event will be easy. You will be calmer, more attune to notice the unexpected, and better equipped to deal with it. Wouldn't we all like to say that our athletes performed well in those adult situations because of the lessons they learned from us?

It's About Humility

Lacrosse is still a growing sport. As a result, in our league, only 3 or 4 of the 16 teams are actually competing for the championship each year. There are years we have won all of the rest of the league games by ten or more goals, sometimes with the second string in for most of the game. There is no pride, no glory, in beating up a team when you are clearly better than they are. You might be better that day, at that sport, but it profits nothing to gloat about it. Stay humble and respect the opponent for coming out to the game.

My first year as a head coach, we made a comeback in the second half of the conference championship game to beat our big rivals. As the clock hit zero and the horn sounded to end the game, I ran out on the field with the team, giving high fives and hugging the seniors while they cheered and congratulated each other. I am not sure how long that went on, but I remember standing in the middle of the field, looking back at the sideline to see our opponents in a line waiting to shake our hands, watching us celebrate. I was embarrassed. I frantically rounded up the team, telling them we would finish the celebration on the bus home, but first, we had to congratulate our opponents on a great game and a great season. It took longer than I would have liked, but eventually, we were in line to shake hands. And I never let that happen again – at least not that badly.

The next time we won the championship, I was able to remind our kids to have more humility in victory. Nearing the end of the game with a large lead, we got all the seniors on the field, and I told the girls on the sideline to go congratulate their teammates at the end of the game, and then come right back to the sideline to shake hands with their opponents. "We'll celebrate on the bus," was the line I kept repeating. That was surprisingly difficult, though. After the game was over, and we had shaken hands, there was an awards ceremony. We got our trophy and took a picture with the championship banner. The girls were being very humble, smiling, holding the trophy, and hugging each other in congratulations. Then the photographer got involved. Not satisfied with the subdued images he was getting, he told the girls to get more excited for the camera. They did, and on the front page of the sports section the following day a few girls were sticking their tongues out and holding the trophy. Being humble was hard. We live in an in-your-face culture. The photographer expected a team that just won a championship to look and behave a certain way, and my girls were not meeting his expectation. Once he encouraged them to strike a boastful pose, they fell easily into that expected role.

I cannot imagine that kind of behavior in any other area of life. When you get a job, you don't run around high fiving your friends, taking selfies with your new contract while all the people you beat out sit and watch. When you get a raise, you don't announce it to the room, smiling and waving it while the people who were let go pack their desks. That kind of behavior would be viewed as incredibly arrogant, inappropriate, and even anti-social. In sports, though, that in-your-face style of celebration is encouraged. It's part of the entertainment value of professional sports, broadcast nationally and praised as the epitome of performance and competition. However, when we are using sports as a way to teach young men and women how to be adults, there is no place for anything more than a hug and a high-five until you are no longer in the presence of your opponent.

This point was really driven home for me during my one season of coaching freshman girls' basketball in a well-to-do suburban town. We had a really talented team, and our varsity team was having a great year. One of our regular league opponents was a school in a rough area of the largest near city. They had a history of fielding great varsity teams for boys' and girls' basketball. For many of us, that was always a reminder of the level playing field that sports offer. The scoreboard on the athletic field does not care how big your house is, the color of your skin, or how much money your parents make. The score always starts 0-0. On that day, though, the group of girls with every socio-economic advantage completely dominated the game.

As I watched the score climb out of control, past the point of subbing out the starters, past the point of the opponent demonstrating frustration and hopelessness, I felt no pride in coaching such a talented team. I only felt embarrassment for beating our opponent so badly. The girls on my team had every advantage over their opponents outside the walls of that gym. They had safe, warm homes, money for plenty of food, clothes, sports camps, private coaching, private academic tutoring, and eventually, expensive private colleges with exclusive alumni networks, and access to the best jobs in interesting careers. For generations, the kids from the city had come out to the suburbs, leaving the crowded, unsafe neighborhoods to see the fields and mansions of suburbia, to the one place they could start on equal footing, but this time, we embarrassed them. And in a way, we embarrassed ourselves. There was no gloating or anything like that, but it just felt *bad*.

Years later, I was in a very similar situation. Like that basketball game, there were culturally charged factors. We were playing a team that drew mostly from their local farming and working class region in an area that didn't really have many opportunities for lacrosse. I drew on my experience in that basketball game to try to avoid the same feeling. To be clear, we are talking about a mismatch so bad that it might have been unsafe to play with the pace and intensity we were used to playing. I believe strongly in having the same standard for every game, regardless of outcome, but this was different. When I realized how bad it was, I called a timeout and told the team to get out of game day mode. Just have fun, make a friend on the other team, and be supportive of them. By the end of the game, our girls were high-fiving the opponent when they made a good play and giving them pointers when they weren't actively playing. Everyone had fun. Our opponents asked us to take pictures together after the game, and the coach wrote us a wonderful thank-you note.

Obviously those are extreme, culturally charged examples, but the lesson holds true in all athletic contests. We might find more success in one game, or one season, or a stretch of seasons, than some of our opponents do, but that does not make us *better* than them. Sure, we should be proud of the work it took to be strong, proud to be part of something that works so well, but we stay humble. We recognize that nothing we have done as athletes or as coaches is solely the product of ourselves. We are boosted or hindered by our circumstances: our parents, our schools, the coaches and teachers we learned from, and often, just by being in the right place at the right time. We teach our athletes to stay humble in victory so they understand that external success does not say anything about the character of the person who achieves it. Character is revealed and built by how you react to your own successes and failures.

It's about Performance

A classic twist on an even more classic cliché goes: *"Sports don't build character; they reveal it."* How you react in the pressure situations that you are put in during athletic contests does, indeed, reveal a lot about you. Performing under that pressure reveals your character, but it is also good practice for building character. It's like any test in school. Most tests do not build your knowledge, but taking the feedback from the test and using it to identify what you do well and areas you can improve does build knowledge, awareness, and yes, character.

Performance during competition is two-dimensional. Executing sport-specific skills and principles is one dimension, but it is equally important to consider how well we express our character.

When considering roles on the team, we begin by asking athletes what they want their teammates, opponents, and fans to say about them at the end of a game, season, or career.

Even when we are not under any pressure, it is well-documented that human beings' reasonable, rational thoughts occur *after* our irrational, emotional, animalistic feelings. The stress and heat of competition will definitely override the conscious choice to demonstrate good sportsmanship, be friendly to your opponents, respectful to the officials, or humble after a big play. It will even override your choice to engage in positive self-talk, to execute your skills, and to play with confidence. A big moment of a big game is overwhelmingly engaging. We cannot think our way through it; we can only perform what we have trained to do. In that moment, character, confidence, and preparation are put to the test. What we do *is* what we have trained to do. Either we perform the way we want to, or we need better training.

One simple example is that I am often tougher on officials than I should be. Every year, I make a point of improving my reactions to calls that do not go our way, and I have made progress, but I am far from good. The heat of the competition overrides my rational intentions and brings out my emotional responses. I know I need to keep working on it, keep training myself by visualizing difficult situations in order to prepare to perform better when they happen in the pressure and urgency of competition. What I did not realize at the beginning of my career was how my actions were also training my athletes.

After a particularly tough, close game, one of my assistant coaches tried to get me to see that. "I don't like the way our kids reacted out there," he explained at halftime. "We sound like a bunch of crybabies." It was a smart, diplomatic way for him to tell me that I needed to cool it with my reactions to officials. I always thought that getting in the referees' ears was a way for me to let my athletes know that I was engaged, that I had their backs. While I do believe that was successful, I did not realize the unfortunate side-effect was that I was also training my athletes to think it was okay to complain about officials' decisions in the middle of a game. I did not *mean* to teach them that, but I did. I trained that into them, so I needed to reverse course and give them new, better training.

Our intentions do not matter, whether for our own behavior or what we teach our athletes. What shows up on game day is what we teach. How many times have you heard a coach yelling at a team, "I taught you how to [insert whatever they *didn't* do properly here]"? When I hear that, I just chuckle. You might have meant to teach them that, but if they didn't do it in the game, you didn't teach it successfully. It doesn't matter what we say or mean to teach. What our athletes do in the heat of competition reveals what we taught them. Our job is to assess how they perform, find the areas where they are lacking, and train them better.

The language we use and the example we set makes a big difference. A lot of coaching is deciding when to say what to whom and how you say it. If I want my athletes to play with poise and confidence, I need to prepare them to do so, and part of how I can do that is in the language I use, in practice as well as games. I started being more vocal about praise and encouragement, saying things like "great fight" when a girl came up with a contested ground ball, or "beautiful transition" when the team moves the ball up the field efficiently. When an individual makes an obvious mistake, I do not scream and yell about how well I taught her to avoid that mistake; I stay silent. There are two reasons for that approach. First, when a player makes an obvious mistake, she knows it. She does not need the coach to be angry about it; she is disappointed in herself. Second, while an athlete may grow to fear that disappointed silence, it is much less likely than any verbalized negative thought to distract the athlete in the heat of the moment. I want my athletes hearing positive thoughts before they have even made the play they are about to make, not being distracted by the anticipation of a negative reaction. That is how I train my athletes to play with confidence. The coaches' language, demeanor, and actions train the athletes as much as their drills, lessons, and lectures. We want to make sure we are sending the right messages. We find out how well we are doing by seeing the athletes perform in games.

Chapter 2

It's Not About The Loss

Losing a game is nothing to be ashamed of, but losing your cool is. Losing track of yourself, your character, and your values because of what the scoreboard says at the end of a game is damaging to yourself and your team. Sometimes, no matter how hard you've worked and how much you deserve it, things just don't go your way on gameday. Losing isn't just about the scoreboard, either. If you create a team culture that isn't overly focused on results, then you are never really measuring yourself against an opponent; you are measuring yourself against your potential.

If we accept the commonly stated but rarely understood premise that coaches are teachers, then the primary goal of a coach is to teach athletes lessons that are transferable to life after sports. In that role, coaches should be excited when they have an opportunity to teach. But you'd be hard pressed to find a coach who gets excited about losing. As a teaching opportunity, though, losing is without equal. Coaches should do everything in their power to win, but when we inevitably do lose a game, we should relish the opportunity to teach important lessons beyond the Xs and Os.

"Losing a game is nothing to be ashamed of, but losing your cool is."

It's About Opportunity

Losing gives coaches the opportunity to teach and athletes an opportunity to learn. When things don't go as planned, successful people don't waste time whining and assigning blame; they honestly assess what happened and what they could have done differently to change the outcome. They take the opportunity to learn. Strategy, the X's and O's, matter in this case. You draw up plays and schemes in order to emphasize the importance of preparation; you make adjustments to emphasize the importance of learning opportunities. If your honest assessment after a loss is that you could have put more emphasis on one strategy or play that was working well, then you adjust.

Even if your emphasis is on tactics of the sport, when you dive into a tactical adjustment instead of getting angry or complaining, the athletes learn resilience, persistence, and reflection. If you decide that you lost because the opponent was superior in one part of the game, then you have an opportunity to work on that part. Losing gives us the feedback we need to better ourselves.

One season, we played a really close game early in the season with a team I really thought we were better than. Okay, so we did not technically lose; we won by two goals, but I felt as though we were a lot better than that. I was measuring against our potential, not our opponent. Honest assessment? We turned the ball over 19 times. Our efficiency on the offensive end was 60% that game, so if we just cut out a third of the turnovers, we would have extended our lead to a comfortable margin, more in line with what I believed to be the difference in the level of play between our two teams.

For the next week, we upped the emphasis on transition play in all different forms in practice. We worked on getting the ball up the field with no defense, catching and passing under pressure, reteaching every option of our clear scheme to develop patience and poise. We took the opportunity to improve, even though we hadn't actually lost. The team has its sights set on a conference championship, and we are holding ourselves to that standard. We were all uncomfortable with letting what we considered to be an average team stay that close to us all game.

We had no way of knowing at the time that we might have underestimated that particular team that season, and that was probably a good thing. The feedback of being that close to what we thought at the time was the middle of the pack in our league gave us a spark, an opportunity to improve that we all wanted to take advantage of. We ended up seeing them in the conference championship six weeks after our first meeting. A lot had changed in that time. We knew that we had dominated every part of the game except for the turnovers last time, and we had developed transition and ball control into a strength. We also beat everyone else in our league – all by more than that tight two-goal margin.

All of our hard work paid off. The rematch in the championship game was one of our most lopsided victories of the season and the largest margin of victory in a championship game in the history of our conference tournament. We turned the ball over only five times, and we won the game 18-5. Fourteen fewer turnovers led to an 11-goal swing in the final score. It happened because, when we turned in a sub-standard performance, we didn't whine or look to blame anyone; we took the opportunity to learn from it. We got better at training in specific tactics and learned to grow from disappointment.

It's About Persistence

Things will not always go your way. You might never get a call to interview for your dream job. Your vacation plans might be canceled or delayed because of storms. Your negotiation for a raise or promotion might be met with a firm "no." Your first idea as an entrepreneur might fail. These are the losses of life. But as the old cliché goes, "Losing is not the end; quitting is the end." You get back to work, do your best, and wait for your next opportunity.

In sports, though, losing can be, quite literally, the end. When the clock ticks down to zero, and you're behind, that's it. It's over. You might not have another chance to beat that team. The coach can always say, "We'll get them next year," but not all the athletes will be back. Losing, especially to a rival, or in some other big game, feels and *is* final. And it's okay to be disappointed about that. It's okay for the bus ride home to be quiet, for some athletes to shed some tears, but it is important that they get over it and get back to work. As coaches, we should be excited to model and teach that because that persistence is a skill our athletes will keep with them into their adult lives.

One season, we lost two regular season games to our biggest rival, giving them five wins over us in two years. Since none of the seniors had been on the varsity team when they were freshmen or sophomores, they never got to win against that big rival. We were simply outmatched in those few years. Our rival won the league all three years and went to the state championship game once. After that sixth straight loss, I tried to put the loss in perspective, but I inadvertently made it worse. "Contrary to popular belief," I began the team address before we started practice the next day, "the sun did rise this morning, even though we lost a lacrosse game." I went on to say that we had another day to work, another day to get better, and that hopefully, we could have another chance to beat that rival in the conference tournament.

I see now that I made two major mistakes in trying to downplay the loss. First, I was focused on the result, not the process. I did *not* say anything about whether we should be proud of our effort or disappointed in an off day. I did not emphasize process *at all* in the way I presented the speech. I talked about losing and the need to move on from the loss because there was a chance that we could win next time. The other mistake was not giving the emotion of the loss enough credit. I did not allow the team to feel the disappointment, to process the loss, internalize the need to improve, and then get back to work. In the same breath, I treated the result of the game as incredibly important - second only to the sun rising - and almost meaningless - expecting them to shake it off and have a great practice so that we could win the next one.

The following season, I had a chance to address the team after another loss to the same league rival, this time in the conference championship game, against a team we could have and should have beaten, extending our losing streak against them to seven games over four seasons. I approached the address to the team from almost the exact opposite angle. "Sometimes, you just don't get what you want," I began, "no matter how hard you've worked or how much you deserve it." I emphasized that I believe this team *did* work hard all season, they did deserve to win, but we did not get it done on the field that night. "It's okay to be disappointed," I said, to validate the feelings of disappointment that come with any missed opportunity. I acknowledged that the seniors would never have another chance to beat the rival and then turned to the lesson they could all get out of the loss: *"Never again will failure feel final,"* I told them, explaining briefly that every failure in the world after sports comes with another chance at success at some point. I encouraged them to spend the rest of the night working through their disappointment but to come back tomorrow ready to put in a good day at practice. "You have done it the right way all season," I explained. "Don't let one loss ruin that." I told the underclassmen to come back and work hard through the next couple weeks because we would get them next year. And we did-twice. In fact, we went on to win the conference championship in each of the next four years.

And for the seniors, I told them to come back ready to work hard as we prepared for a tough run in the state championship tournament because, even though we were going to face a very tough opponent in the first round, that persistence is what they will take with them when they are done with sports. Never again will a failure feel as permanent as it does when the clock ticks down to 0 in a championship game. If you can process that disappointment and then remain persistent through that kind of failure, then you'll have no problem being persistent in your life after sports.

When you lose, you might learn some things about your team and what you need to work on. It's the coach's job to point those things out and teach persistence. A loss is not necessarily a reason to run more or get tougher in practice. A loss is a reason to teach persistence. If you lost because you were out-run in the last few minutes of the game, then yes, running more in practice is an appropriate response. But persistence is steady, not impulsive. Persistence means making small adjustments based on feedback but continuing to believe in yourself, not losing track of your values and changing everything or just getting angry and changing nothing. If you don't get a promotion, you look for opportunities to get more relevant experience, so you'll be in a better position next time that promotion rolls around. If you lose a game, you look for opportunities to improve in the areas where you were outmatched. You don't make drastic, impulsive changes. You stay the course, work hard, and know that with a little improvement every day, your persistence will pay off.

In sports, it does not have to pay off with a later win. Your record might not be any better in any given season because of the persistence you taught your athletes. But the emphasis on process will not only be better for them in teaching long-term lessons, but it will make practice more enjoyable, more purposeful. When the emphasis is on persistence, the athletes can get back into the flow of engaging in practice, and that will help them get over the disappointment of the loss in a healthy, productive way.

It's About Pride

After most losses, working as hard as you can the next day is important because there is another game to get ready for, hence the importance of persistence, but when seniors lose their last game, that's it. There is no next game to prepare for; their high school careers are over. Unless they are among the few who go on to the college level, they will have no other opportunities to play for that championship, no other results-oriented reason to practice their sport. The coach can always say, "We'll get them next year," and get back to work, but not all of the athletes will have that chance. So for those who will never play again, what good comes from losing?

I have never coached a season that ended with a win. If you're any good, almost every season ends with a loss in the postseason. Hopefully, one of those years, you will win it all. You can take immense pride that, but that cannot happen every year to every team. You need to be prepared to lose every year, for your seniors to leave the field upset or disappointed on their last day playing the sport. We can teach them to take pride in their efforts by the way we frame that loss, but also each day in practice, as we emphasize growth and effort, giving them something to be proud of when they walk off the field for the last time.

As coaches, our job is to make sure that level of effort is there every day, so that when we say those things after losses, we are telling the truth. We teach our athletes to take pride in their practice, to get a little better each day, and we stay on top of them about it in practice, so that when it's all over, we can honestly say they should be proud.

My second year as a head coach, we had a very strong team. I was so excited about our potential that I never prepared to lose. When we lost a close game to a perennial rival in the state tournament, I was completely unprepared. The team met at the center of the field, and we all just kind of sat there for a while. They needed me to give them something, but I was not prepared; I did not expect to lose, and I did not have the experience to do anything but sit there with them, disappointed that the season was over too soon. Both of my assistant coaches, who had more experience with good coaches at a higher level of athletics as an athlete than I ever did, started talking about remembering all four years, but they, also surprised and inexperienced, did not quite articulate what they meant either. So we sat there, disappointed, and eventually went our separate ways home.

What the other coaches were getting at, and what I wish I had been able to say at the time, was that there was no shame in losing that game. That it was okay to be disappointed, but they should be proud of everything they accomplished that season, and the seniors for all four years. That was a great team. They won the conference championship three years in a row and had given a fantastic effort in their last game. The team that beat us that game is a perennial powerhouse. Our in-season rivalry has spanned three decades, and we have never beaten them. There is no shame in losing to that team. We should have walked off that field proud of the effort we put in, proud with the knowledge that we did the absolute best we could that day - which we did - in the days leading up to that game, every day that season, and every day for the four years the seniors were there.

Losing a game is a good checkpoint for your pride. In a successful season, you can ask yourself, have you gotten a little too prideful? Have you let the results go to your head, losing track of your process? Or, have you continued to work hard, do the best you can, every practice and every game, but run into an opponent who was just better? The answers to those questions are much more important than the score at the end of a game or the record at the end of a season. If you have put your all into each practice, each game, the whole season, then you can walk off the field after that last game proud of what you have accomplished. Even if that is internal, even if your results on the scoreboard are not going to attract any reporters or accolades, you can be proud of yourself, your team, and the progress you made.

Chapter 3

It's Not About The Team

When coaches emphasize the importance of the team, they risk sending the message that each athlete's value depends entirely on his contribution to the team. He acts for the good of the team. That mentality can motivate some people some of the time. People will work harder when they feel they are part of something "greater and more permanent than themselves," but the team structure of competitive high school sports has so much more to offer than that. Of course, learning to put team achievement before individual accolades is an important lesson in the relationship among pride, humility, sacrifice, and achievement, but those are topics for another chapter. In a more significant way, the team provides each athlete with a sense of identity, camaraderie, and support of his or her peers. In those ways, the team acts for the immediate and long-term benefit of each individual, and a coach should structure the team to promote and take advantage of that.

It's About Support

During one of our strongest seasons, one of our strongest players was going through a really hard time. Katie's[1] inner struggles had led her to isolate herself from many of her teammates, who did not seem interested in talking to her about anything that did not help them get focused on lacrosse. As a result, she turned to outside friends, eventually missing practices, creating a cycle of further disconnect from the athletes and coaches she used to rely on. With my team-centered mentality, I thought she was not doing her part for the team, so she did not deserve the privilege of full participation on it. I punished her with lost playing time and spoke with her about importance of being on time and working hard at every practice. I did not ask her the reasons for her change in behavior; I just made it clear that it was not good for the team. By doing so, I reinforced the message that her value to the team depended on how much effort she put in to make herself valuable on the field. That meant showing up on time, putting in a strong effort in practice, and performing on the field. End of story.

That one-sided approach was seriously detrimental in this case and only led to Katie further distancing herself, missing more practice time and more game time. It all came to a head the day of one of our biggest games, when she called one of the captains asking for a ride

---

[1] Name changed

to the bus. She was not staying at home, having been kicked out of her parents' house the night before. The captain was furious that Katie had chosen to stay out at someone's house the night before a big game and asked her why she did not call one of her teammates in that time of need. She didn't have a good answer, but I quickly came to understand what she probably couldn't articulate in that moment. She didn't call because her teammates – led by me, her coach - had not demonstrated that we would be there for her. The team was not there for her, to support her. She was dealing with adversity far beyond the thrill of victory and the agony of defeat, but I was absorbed - lost, maybe, or worse, obsessed - with building a team that would succeed on the field, rather than developing people who would succeed in life. Without ever saying it, I sent the message that the team was only there for you if you were focused on the team. Katie didn't have the energy to focus on the team, but she needed us to be there for her.

It is easy for high school kids to get lost in disproportionate reactions to meaningless or insignificant problems: cliques, dating, friends, and the outcomes of sporting events. The team's leaders, coach first, should always be looking to help, support, and offer guidance. We should never be angry with our athletes. We should understand that the mistakes they make on and off the field are part of their growing up and maturation. Coaches can have a profound impact on that maturation process if we guide and support athletes through those mistakes. Unfortunately, we can also be, as I was for Katie, a source of additional confusion and stress in an already confusing and stressful time.

After that game, Katie made an appointment with me and explained some of the things that had been going on. I apologized for not being more sensitive to her life outside of sports and encouraged her to come back to the team at her own pace, but the damage was done. She eventually quit the team without even telling anyone. She just stopped showing up.

What I learned, unfortunately too late to help Katie, is that the athlete has to get something out of being on the team besides the cliché, "Being part of something bigger than yourself." What that "something" is matters. Is it a winning machine with a long history of on-the-field success? Or is it a community of like-minded individuals who share a love of their sport and who grow to love each other? Most teams are neither; few can be both. But it is far more effective to start with community and build from there than to start with winning – to try to build a machine out of people.

It's About the Individual

A coach educates individuals. The team is the learning environment, not the pupil. The team changes every year, but the athletes stay for four. Every year, the team will look a little different. The only constant, in the long run, is the coach. Coaches, intentionally or unintentionally, by preaching a team-centered mindset, sometimes create a coach-centered mindset. The message is almost never intentional, but it's clear to anyone who takes a moment to think about it. It's not really about the team; it's about the coach.

In the midst of a disappointing season, we were behind a team we had not lost to in several years and certainly should have beaten that year. At halftime, I got tough, telling the kids that I had heard the word among our opponents that we were not the invincible team they used to be afraid of anymore. "I own too much black and gold," I finished, "for this team not to be what it used to be." I'm not sure what I was trying to accomplish. I think I was just venting.

All I accomplished was to make the success of the team about *me*. It was not about the people on the team and not even something more benign, like tradition or pride. I made it dead clear in that moment that being successful as a team, carrying on the tradition of the program on the field, was a reflection on me. We lost that game, never really mounting much of a comeback effort, and I never felt that I was able to get that team to buy in again. We finished the season weakly, posting a losing record for the first time in a decade and the only losing season I had at that school.

A lot of the reason for the lack of on-the-field success that season was that I miscalculated that teams' appreciation for the tradition that came before them. That halftime moment of a bad loss was symptomatic of my approach the whole season. In that moment, I said probably the most damaging thing I could to a group following three of the most successful seasons in the history of the program. The individuals on that team were never confident that they could carry the torch, nor should they have been. Our level of dominant success in our conference could not last forever. Eventually, one season, a team wasn't going to win the conference championship. In a lot of ways, we all knew there was a good chance it would be that team, and they were crushed under the pressure of trying to live up to something they could not be. They wanted to be themselves: a group of individuals who were very good at the sport. Instead, they felt like robots, expected to fill in mindlessly for the group before them, to match the success of the previous years, to further the tradition of winning that they did not start and did not necessarily want. That year, appealing to the team or the history of the program as a "greater good" backfired. It was not the right approach for that moment.

That is not to say that there is never an appropriate time to appeal to history and tradition. In fact, the team the previous season, the one that won the third-straight conference championship, was ready and excited for the challenge. One of the captains of that team became a coach, and we stayed connected. Years after she graduated, she told me that her mentality, which she spread to the rest of the team, was: "We are not going to the be team that breaks the streak." That was part of the challenge she and her teammates were willing to take on because doing so was part of their self-image. So if being part of a tradition matters to the individual, then that can be a good motivator. It is never wrong to appeal to an individual athlete's sense of self.

The year after the debacle described above, I started a new tradition, but it had nothing to do with championship banners and cheers left over from decades ago. In February, as we started putting together pre-season workouts and setting team goals, I took all the seniors out to dinner. The goal was to hang out, talk about the season, and talk as a group about each team member. We told them what they did well, why they were appreciated as a valuable member of the team, what they should focus on in the coming season, and what they should expect in terms of playing time, position, and goals. It was not me telling the kids what I think; almost all of the conversation came from their teammates. Since I started that tradition, it has been an unvaryingly positive experience, setting the stage for a team of individuals who are encouraged to be themselves. They know that their individual development and accomplishment is important to the team. That is one way to communicate that the team exists for the good of the people that participate on it.

Every year, the team is new. Some athletes graduate, leaving holes that need to be filled by returning or new athletes. Each year, each individual on the team will have a different role to play, different expectations and different goals. Developing and communicating those expectations and goals to each individual is essential to the learning experience and leads to happier, more productive teams, which in turn, leads to more winning.

It's About Roles

In competitive sports, "role player" is often a euphemism for a player who just isn't very good: someone who gets limited playing time, usually at the end of a blowout. On any team, though, everyone has a role, whether it is explicitly stated or unspoken and implied. One of the great benefits of the senior dinner described above is that each member of the senior class got to hear what her teammates needed and expected from her, so everyone was on the same page. There was no risk of athletes being unsure of their role or their importance to the team.

When I first became a head coach, I had the mixed blessing of inheriting one of the best classes of lacrosse players ever to play together at that school. There were several girls on the team who were talented in multiple aspects of the game, and they all tried to do it all. Their senior year, some jealousy broke out over who was scoring goals at what times. The team did not play to its potential because none of the best players had clearly defined roles. After that class graduated, no one was sure what to expect. We had plenty of talented girls coming back but no one who could compete with the top three or four who graduated. To even come close to our matching the success of the previous two seasons, we would need to get a little bit more out of every single player on the field. And that's how every girl on the team became a role player.

What I learned from the years with and after that underperforming class was that, even the most capable athletes need to have clearly defined roles. Because no one in the class that followed them had the ability to "do it all," I spent time thinking about what each athlete *could* do. What could I tell each kid to focus on so they contributed the most they could to the team effort? I met with assistants, came up with roles for each athlete, and we set out to play a true team game, where some girls focused on possession, some on scoring, some on hustle, and some on simply cheering the team on or working the starters hard in practice.

The result? The clearly less talented team had the best record in the history of the school (a record that was broken three years later by a team that had both the talent and the defined roles). We went to the state championship game for the first time in the history of our program. And at the banquet, I credited the success to the willingness of each individual to be a role player and to get really good at her role. I explained in front of the families in attendance what each athlete contributed. That was easy because we communicated about it all year. Their roles, and the appreciation the coaches and players felt for them, was genuine. It was not difficult to come up with meaningful roles; it just took some time, collaboration, and communication.

In any gathering of people working toward any goal, everyone has *something* to offer. Even the athlete that can do it all can't do it all *all the time*. Everyone has to know what he is good at, develop their strengths, take pride in their contribution. The lasting lesson that athletes should learn from being on a team is not something as simple or cliched as, "Make sacrifices for a greater good," or "Be part of something bigger than yourself." They should learn that being on a team means contributing what you can, as well as you can, and taking pride in that contribution. That's the lesson that applies to life after sports.

Finding a role for everyone is the job of the coach, but it can't be totally controlled by the coach. The athlete has to have some input into her role. If she does not get a say in her role, if she does not feel any ownership of it, then she is just doing what the coach says. She is, like the team that underperformed because I made their success about *me*, a mechanical object filling a role the coach put her in. If she has input, then she is doing what she wants to do. She is a multi-dimensional, sentient person *ful*filling a role of her choosing, not filling a role because an authority figure said so. It is the coach's job to develop a team made up of all those people.

That doesn't mean the athlete simply dictates her role. The role is a compromise, the result of collaboration among athlete, teammates, and coaches. A girl who is in the bottom half of the team in endurance running is not going to be a starting midfielder. If she thinks she is, it is the coach's responsibility to explain that she is not, and why she is not, and find another role she is willing to perform. These conversations can be tough, but clear communication about expectations up front will save a lot of headaches later in the season. When you think of teams as a collection of role players, you build a team around your athletes, instead of fitting the athletes to your team. That subtle difference pays big dividends in motivation, team culture, and eventually, on-the-field accomplishment.

It's About Responsibility

The phrase "take responsibility" usually has a connotative connection with wrongdoing. A politician takes responsibility for a mistake

"In any gathering of people working toward any goal, everyone has something to offer. Even the athlete that can do it all can't do it all all the time. Everyone has to know what he is good at, develop his strengths, take pride in his contribution."

caused by government bureaucracy, or a coach takes responsibility for a loss. However, responsibility can and should be approached in a much more positive way. When athletes know their roles, they have the opportunity to take responsibility for them, and the coach and the team have the obligation to hold them accountable to that responsibility.

On the field, that is easy. As long as the athletes know what their roles are, they should want to take responsibility for them. If one athlete has been identified as a possession attacker, she knows she is responsible for catching every ball that comes near her and making good decisions, throwing low-risk passes to open teammates in space. On the other hand, a girl who is identified as more of a scoring threat is responsible for taking more risks. She should be willing to throw a slightly risky pass to a teammate that might score or take on the opponent's best defender in a one on one because it is her responsibility to take calculated risks that lead to goals. There are, of course, countless other responsibilities that need to be taken care of on the field that add up to a successful day, and those responsibilities might be different on every team, based on the specific strengths and weaknesses of the individuals that make up the team.

But responsibilities to the team extend off the field, as well. If an athlete does not get much playing time, she knows she has a supporting role. It is her responsibility to tell her teammate, "It's okay," when she appears distressed about a mistake or shout, "Way to go," when a player on the field makes a great play. Those roles are important and should be treated as such by the coaches and teammates.

One time, I asked the captains to send some people out to get food from my car for a team meal. I was dismayed to see that all of the

freshmen were coming out. It is *not* the freshmen's responsibility to do the grunt work in our program. Everyone does their share. That is a standard that I am pretty clear about, and it applies to setting up practice, keeping track of equipment, and everything else. So, when we got inside and set up the food, I said to the team, "I assume that because the freshmen came out to get the food, we are going to let them eat first. Because we are not a team that makes freshmen do extra work just because they are freshmen." I caught one of the captain's eye. She smirked, nodded, and said, "Yeah, you're right. Freshmen get your food." The next time I asked for help bringing food in, there were random representatives from every class there.

Because the older you get, the more responsibility you should have, seniors have more responsibility than freshmen, because they know and are used to the standards. They help pick up the equipment and set up for practice alongside the freshmen, while also serving as mentors and guides for younger teammates. Captains have the responsibility of being a liaison between the athletes and the coaches, organizing team building activities so everyone feels included and setting the tone for every practice and game. Here, responsibility merges with support. If the captains are doing all of that, but then saying "freshmen do it" whenever something menial needs to be done, then the team is seeing them *not* taking responsibility. The team won't see the work that goes into the deeper stuff. The meetings with coaches, the planning that goes into each team event. That's all

behind the scenes. What they see is that the captains take responsibility for picking up equipment alongside everyone else. They lead by example and pull the team along with them.

Coaches have to do the same thing. Most athletes will have no idea how much work it is to lead a program - all the little things a coach does to build the experience for the student athletes. Or if they do, they'll only notice the mistakes. So you have to be willing to take on menial responsibilities too, responsibilities that are more visible, so the team doesn't just know you are there to help them, they observe you doing it.

It's About Accountability

The flip side of responsibility is accountability, and there is far more to accountability than yelling at athletes or taking away playing time. Accountability, like responsibility, can be a positive, athlete-driven concept. Etymologically, "account-ability" comes from the ability to account for something, which means to keep track of it. With this understanding, any way an athlete can check up on how well she is taking responsibility for her role can lend accountability. That might mean occasional quick check-ins with a captain or coach, answering one question: How did you take responsibility for your role in practice this week? If one of the roles an athlete took on was to always treat opponents with respect, she might report that she helped an opponent up after an accidental collision or that she reminded her teammates to stop carrying on on the bench during the late stages of a non-competitive game. Or she might report that she failed to do one of those things, or worse, was so upset after a loss she did not shake an opponent's hand. That does not mean she serves some kind of punishment for that. Simply realizing the mistake is being accountable. If the individuals on the team take responsibility for their roles, then realizing when they have failed to fulfill those roles holds them accountable. Running, losing playing time, and other punitive strategies often masquerade as methods of accountability, but they are just punishments. Punishment is not wrong, but it needs to be used carefully, deliberately, and sparingly. Accountability, like responsibility, is about communication, preparation, and reflection. It does not require punishment to be effective.

In the same way, taking a kid out of a game can be seen as punishment or accountability, but there is an important distinction. Let's go back to our two girls with almost opposite roles: the possession attacker and the risk-taking attacker. If the possession attacker drops a few passes or throws an ill-advised pass, it might be appropriate to take her out of the game. In the same way, if the risk-taker starts playing too safe, looking like she is afraid to make a mistake, she might come out, too. The difference between punishment and accountability is what happens next. If it's about punishment, the coach says something like, "Get your head in the game," or something perhaps a bit more colorful, as the athlete jogs to the bench to get a drink of water, where she waits until called upon to be trusted not to screw up again. If it's about accountability, the coach takes a little more time speaking to the individual and the specifics of her role. For the risk taker, the coach asks her what she's seeing that has made her slow down, reminds her that her role is to take risks when they are likely to make good things happen, and get her back on the field. For the possession player, the same applies. The coach reminds her that the team trusts her to see the defense and make smart passes, asks what led to the mistake. While the role an athlete takes is personal, unique to her, the accountability is individual but never personal. Accountability is about understanding what went wrong and preparing to correct it the next chance you get.

It's About Priorities

When I was growing up, my parents, teachers, coaches, and other adults had always told me that I could be anything I wanted, that I could do anything I wanted. The first time I ever had to make a major sacrifice, to choose one direction at the sacrifice of the other, was when I entered high school, and I had to make a very difficult choice between golf and baseball. My two best sports were both spring sports. I had such a difficult time choosing that for a time I thought I could try to do both. Eventually, I decided to give up baseball and join the golf team. Of course, looking back on it, I know that doing both, or at least doing both well, would have been impossible. I would have had to miss team events for both sports and would not have been fully part of either. If for some reason I had been allowed to be a part of both teams, I would not have benefitted from any of the long-term lessons I discuss in this book. So I had to choose. I thought at the time that I was making a huge sacrifice, making a decision that would shape my high school experience, choosing one road and never being able to go back and choose the other. How fortunate I am that my choice was about something as safe as what sport to play. I got to practice making important decisions about priorities, but the consequences of the decision were minimal. I joined the golf team, was a four-year starter and two-year captain. Once I made that choice, I never really missed baseball. My life would have been different, sure. If I had chosen baseball, I might have had different friends, different experiences, and those probably could have been good friends and good experiences, but I am happy with the friends and experiences I had. The important lesson I learned was to choose a priority and commit to it. Making that choice wasn't easy, but it was an important part of my growth from adolescence to adulthood. It wasn't the decision I made that helped me grow; it was the fact that I *had* to make that decision.

That is why coaches demand long hours, don't allow athletes to miss practices for other clubs, off-season sports, or social events. We want our athletes to understand the benefit of committing to something fully, even when that commitment costs you something. The athlete might miss out on hanging out with her friends one or two Friday nights because of games. She might have to skip the concert that her friends are going to because practice ends too late to get there. Coaches are not holding firm about those sacrifices because we want control of our athletes or our teams; we are holding firm because we want to teach our athletes the importance of committing to something, especially when that means sacrificing something else. That is an important lesson in setting and sticking to priorities. The practice of prioritizing sports is important because there are real but minor consequences to the decisions you make. And when you commit fully to an experience, it is far richer and more rewarding. If you're not committed, you're just playing games.

Life is full of difficult choices with much farther reaching consequences than a missed concert or night with your friends. I sacrificed something when I gave up baseball. I missed out on a life experience, but I prioritized and committed to a different one: golf. What I lost was small, but it was real. That's why I call it practice. At some point, you have to sacrifice something in order to have something else. Sacrifice the nicer car so you can go on vacation or vice versa. Committing to team sports teaches us that it will be okay. The sacrifices we make pale in comparison to what we gain by fully committing to our priorities.

You can do anything, but you can't do *everything*.

One day, one of our senior All-American captains missed a practice. Even worse, it was the day before a game. It was the biggest game of the year, the league tournament game against our biggest rival, whom we beat in the regular season game a week before but was certainly a formidable opponent. The captain told me well in advance what she was doing that day. Because of her enthusiasm for lacrosse and her scholarship to play division 1 the next year, she was at the Lacrosse Final Four. She told me she was going, and we thought she would be

47

back in time for practice. But she wasn't. She did everything right, calling when she got behind to say she would probably miss practice.

At our school, if you miss practice the day before a game, you cannot start in the next game. That's a department-wide rule, non-negotiable. When I addressed the team about the game, I made it clear that one of our captains was going to be sitting for the first possession of the game because she has a responsibility to follow the rules, just like every other player, and I have a responsibility as a coach to follow the rules, just like the players do. It was a good opportunity for me to let everyone know that, when they serve those kind of punishments, it's nothing personal. At times, punishments are appropriate ways to address problems (see more on that in the section on punishment), and that never means that the coaches don't like you.

It doesn't matter what your role is, whether you are the all-time leading scorer on our team (which this captain was), or a JV player whose role is to work on taking shots with your non-dominant hand in games so you develop that confidence for the future. Accountability happens when a person realizes she has failed to take responsibility for her role.

"You can do anything, but you can't do everything."

Chapter 4

It's Not About Control

I once met a high-performing, very experienced coach who lamented at times that he wished he never left the high school coaching ranks, not because of the pressure or expectations of the college level, but because his college athletes always wanted to know *why* they should do things; high school kids were satisfied just knowing *how*. Yes, having to explain the rationale behind everything you do can be exhausting, but wouldn't we rather raise a generation to ask "why?" than be satisfied with knowing "how"? It's the difference between, "How does a combustible engine work?" and "Why can't cars run on electricity?" If coaches take their roles as educators seriously, then the whole point of every rule, technique, and play is *why*. We want our athletes to be mentally active, invested in the sport and the program. Giving them some autonomy, encouraging them to ask "why?" can be a powerful way to get the buy-in we are looking for. It also allows us to reflect on our philosophies and practices. If we can't or don't want to answer "why?" maybe we need to change.

It's About Discipline

Although it may not be clear from the way the words are used in athletics and education, discipline is not synonymous with punishment. Punishment is a reaction; discipline is a state of mind. Yet I frequently hear teachers, administrators, and coaches use the words interchangeably. Perhaps thinking "punish" sounds harsh and less official, administrators say, "We will have to discipline" some person or group for some wrongdoing. What they really mean is that the offending party is going to serve some kind of punishment: sprints, detention, suspension, or perhaps something more creative. Those authority figures are using discipline as a softer way to say "punish," but in doing so, they could miss the point of what discipline actually is.

Discipline is a set of behaviors that result from well-communicated expectations for behavior, including communicating *why* that behavior is important. The well-disciplined team is rarely punished. They understand the role of the team in their lives, the role of themselves on their team, and the reason that team standards exist. In fact, they probably had at least some say in what those rules and procedures would be. They *want* to live up to the standards because they either made them up or have a full understanding of where they come from. They rarely, if ever, need to be punished for breaking them.

By getting involved in the town youth program, I get to know a lot of the athletes who will play for me, and they get to know me. With my assistant coaches and current high school players, I run winter clinics, summer camps, and other events for the youth organization. When I run clinics, I often take the time to explain what we do at the high school level and why we do it that way.

One example is the way I want them to line up their sticks at the start of practice. I explain that when they arrive, they should get their equipment on right away, and they can pass with someone or shoot around on an open cage before the whistle blows to signal it's time to stretch. When that whistle sounds, they line their sticks up parallel to each other, head on the sideline, and put their mouth guard and goggles in the head of the stick. *Why?* Because then, as soon as they are done stretching, they can get that equipment back on and get ready for the first drill right away. It is efficient and saves wasted time they might otherwise spend tripping over sticks and picking through equipment to find their things.

The first time I explain it at each clinic, I elaborate, explaining the time that is lost over a whole season if they have to dig in their bag to find something after stretching. That lost time, if spent in one of the high-intensity stickwork drills we do at the start of every practice, adds up to so many catches and throws that if they are not ready, they won't be as good as they could have been if they were ready. They understand the reason for that standard, and they know how it benefits *them*; it's not just a rule the coach came up with to have control over a team.

What you communicate to your players matters and creates a culture of deliberate behavior, not just rule following. The significance of just of how much my athletes pick up from me hit me at one of those winter clinics, when a sophomore, Gina, was working with a group of young youth players in an eight-minute station rotation. As I let the coaches know that the eight-minute clock had started, the group that was heading to Gina was only about halfway through their 30-yard walk to her station. "Come on, jog over," Gina yelled out in a friendly but authoritative way. "We're wasting precious practice time!" It was not a rule for that clinic that everyone start exactly at the start of the clock or that the high school girls were in charge of getting the girls to their stations on time. Gina made a decision based on the culture that she understood. She did not behave based on a series of rules handed down to her from a coach. She made decisions based on the values the coaches and older players communicated. Practice time is valuable, and every player should be getting better every minute. With that understanding, she knew the right thing to do was to tell them to jog between stations. It wasn't a rule; it was an example of discipline.

It's About Motivation

When I was a young, inexperienced coach, I inherited a very talented, very successful team. A mentor gave me some advice to keep them from becoming complacent: "Keep dangling the carrot." He did not explain exactly what that meant, and at first, I wanted to dismiss it as a "tough love" alpha-male approach. As I interpreted it, there was an implied second half to that advice: "Never let them get it." Because I could not make much more sense of it, I forgot about it. I encouraged and praised the great athletes, and we won a lot of games, but we got complacent. At that time in my career, I did not know enough about the game to know what carrots to dangle. Two of those athletes went on to have very successful Division-I careers, and most of the rest played at some level in college. I had a team full of athletes with bright college careers ahead of them, and all I could do was tell them, "Nice job."

During the first days of that first season, one of the best girls who ever played for us, Kendra, approached me after practice and asked what she should be working on to keep getting better. I didn't realize it then, but I was out of carrots. I cringe to think of it now, but I actually said, "You're doing great. I'm more concerned about getting the bottom half of our starting lineup to be ready for games, so I really haven't been watching you much. Just keep doing what you're doing." She ended up being a successful division one athlete, no thanks to that advice.

Years later, I had a similar team, consisting of multiple Division-I caliber players, all of whom were highly focused and dedicated. We practiced with intensity and had great success in games. And I always knew what to say next. I knew enough about the game and had enough experience coaching it to bring out carrot after carrot. I congratulated them when they showed marked improvement, while always giving them another carrot to reach for, another skill, tactic, or concept to master. Dangling the carrot does not mean keeping a reward out of reach. It means giving athletes direction and always having another step, another level, ready to dangle for them when they are ready. I encouraged them be proud of what they'd accomplished but never satisfied with where they were. On that team, no one got complacent. One girl, Lindsay, was the league player of the year as a junior, and she got a lot better for her senior year. Another girl, Emily, beat out for player of the year by Lindsay their junior year, got even better, improving in every area, getting more physical, and adding an entire set of skills to her game. Emily was voted player of the year that season. Both were All-Americans, and both left with Division-I scholarships.

Of course, for Kendra, Lindsay, and Emily, like all great athletes, their individual drive to improve was mostly responsible for their success. All the girls from that first team had that same drive, and they improved a lot, even without my help. The difference is, with Kendra's team, I just got out of their way and cheered them on. With Lindsay and Emily, I always had another carrot in my pocket. I could keep the top performers reaching for another level from the day they stepped on the field until the day they went to college. I wonder how much better Kendra could have been and how much more success the team could have had, if I had understood how to push them properly. That first year, we lost a heartbreaker in the state quarterfinals against a team we really thought we could beat. When Lindsay and Emily were seniors, we cruised through the regular season and tournament conference championships, amassing a 20-2 record, and lost in the state finals to a team that would have been really tough to beat.

It's About Process

When I did not have much experience as a coach, the only way I knew how to judge performance was by results. We either won or lost. You either scored a goal or the goalie made the save. The only carrot I had in mind was the result. But when you are playing competitive team sports, the results are not reliable indicators of performance. You can take a great shot, but a goalie makes a spectacular save; you can play a great game but lose to a more talented team. As coaches, we need to understand that improving anything is a process. If we emphasize the process, we de-emphasize the external rewards, and we keep our athletes focused on the next carrot. We do not need our teams to do everything exactly as we tell them; we need them to do it a little better today than they did yesterday. That is how we keep them motivated, whether we are undefeated state champions or at the bottom of our league.

On any given day, to win a game against a team that is equal to you, you need to control possession, win the turnover or loose ball game, and probably get a couple lucky bounces to go your way, as well. You can't control all those things on any given day. What you can control is the discipline of your offense and the level of hustle you exhibit. If those things remain constant regardless of results, the results will be favorable more often than not. A coach has very little control over the outcome of any one particular game.

Athletes, like everyone else, are not best off when they are working for external rewards. Even praise and high-fives are rewards and can be given too freely. When I first began coaching, my strategy was to give them confidence and get out of their way, rewarding them with praise when they succeeded. While there is a time and place for that approach, it was not a deliberate strategy at the time. It was a necessity of my limited knowledge of the sport. I could not give them constructive feedback because I did not know what they could do to get better.

Years later, my approach was very different. My athletes would still describe me as a calm coach who gives a lot of positive feedback, but that is now deliberate, and I have a lot more constructive direction - new carrots to chase - for the top performers. That adds up to a huge benefit to the team as a whole. When the reserves and JV kids see the All-Americans working hard, developing new abilities right through the end of their high school careers, they are more apt to stay focused, too. Each kid has a different carrot to chase, and each is encouraged to chase her own. That does not mean a coach should never praise or reward an athlete for reaching that carrot, just that a coach needs to put the carrot in plain sight by communicating what it is the athlete needs to do to improve and always know what the next carrot will be. That is how we keep process at the center of our athlete's experience. The results will follow the process.

It's About Engagement

Engagement is more than focus on a task. Engagement is extended focus, task after task, or step after step, on a long-term goal – or even more accurately, focus on the process of building to a long-term goal. It ranks among the most transferable and important skills we can teach our athletes. In order to engage your athletes in practice, games, or the team, you, the coach, must be engaged. The old cliché is true: "They don't care how much you know until they know how much you care." That means caring for each individual but also for the sport and the team. And it's not enough to tell them you care; you have to show it. You show it by being energetic in practice, giving specific feedback to individuals, and being genuinely excited when they take that feedback and improve. You engage athletes when you command attention. Not demand - command. Athletes are not engaged because you demand that they pay attention, yelling at them or threatening them with punishment if they lose focus. That is a coach demanding attention. Commanding attention means creating an exciting, energetic environment that athletes want to be engaged in. In many ways, that piece of engagement goes hand in hand with the concept of flow. Athletes need to be pushed just beyond their limits, asked to do things that do not come readily or easily, but are not out of reach. When coaches are energetic, available, and genuinely invested in what each player is doing, we give our athletes the best chance to be engaged: to experience flow.

I have always been an energetic, enthusiastic, supportive coach, but it took me a while to learn to be as engaged as I describe the term above. For a while, my basic coaching strategy was to shout encouragement and get out of the way of the athletes. In a lot of ways, that worked. It created upbeat, engaging practices and a game environment in which athletes were not too busy listening to me to be engaged in the game. But we can do more to engage our athletes. I was not fully engaged because I was not paying enough attention to each individual's experience. I was caught in a mindset of managing a team, not coaching individuals, so I missed a lot of opportunities to engage with those individuals, to prove I cared and help them reach their potential.

One game, one of the strongest, smartest players I have ever coached, Brittany, was having an off day. She came off the field frustrated, and, not knowing how to handle it, I simply slapped her hand and said, "Good hustle," as she went to the bench to get a drink. I did not mean it. She was not hustling particularly well that day. If anything, her frustration was weighing on her, and she looked slower than usual. I was searching for something positive to say in hopes that she would break out of her frustration. It backfired. Brittany saw through the comment because it was not genuine feedback. From her perspective, she saw a coach not paying any attention, not engaged. She knew she was having an off day, and she needed me to engage in that experience with her, to tell her that I saw it, and would support her or push her through the difficult day. By doing so, I could have sent a contagious example of engagement. Instead, I sent a message of disengagement through meaningless praise.

It gets worse from there. I did not just miss a chance to engage; I seriously damaged the long-term relationship and culture. "Good hustle?" I overheard Brittany say to a teammate as she took a sip of her water. It was what came next that I will never forget: "Does he even *like* me?" I was so stunned that I never addressed that.

Of course I liked her. As I said, she was one of the best athletes and smartest kids I ever coached. It was because I liked her that I tried to spare her feelings by giving her meaningless praise instead of honest feedback, but she had no way of knowing that. To her, it seemed that I was not paying attention to her, was not engaged in her performance, or the game, or her life. My effort to be *nice* because I didn't want to upset her appeared to her as a lack of any effort at all. When she saw I was not engaged, she took it very personally. She needed me to show that I cared, that I was engaged, by giving her honest feedback. When I didn't, she thought it was because I didn't care about her.

Our athletes do not want us to be *nice*; they need us to be engaged, to be fully present during practice, games, and their lives off the field. They want honest feedback, including criticism. When you make it clear that you are engaged, that you care about them and believe in them, you will see them make amazing progress. If you resort to a few stock phrases of praise and criticism or try to spare their feelings, like I did, athletes can disconnect, losing engagement with you and the sport, and never reach their potential.

"Commanding attention means creating an exciting, energetic environment that athletes want to be engaged in."

It's About Problem Solving

Even the best coaches, who have instilled the best cultures, will run into problems. In those cases, our actions as coaches must come from a desire to teach how to prevent problems, not simply punish problem-causers. Early in my career, I heard a lot of experienced coaches say that running is never an appropriate punishment.

Punishing athletes by making them run only works in the sense of a "rule by fear" approach and turns athletes off to one of the most important things they can do to train for just about any sport. Okay, so we don't want to use running as a punishment. But it is so often the only thing that works immediately, that draws attention to any problem and holds athletes accountable to fixing that problem. So I continued to use running as punishment because I just hadn't seen any good alternatives.

Eventually, though, I came to rethink the purpose and methods of punishing athletes. What do we really want when we punish? We want to discourage a behavior; we want athletes to be accountable to something they have done wrong. When we resort to running as a punishment, we are teaching our athletes to think two things: "Coach is in charge," and "Running is not something I should ever want to do." While the first thought is not necessarily a bad lesson in the right context, there is no sport in which athletes should be mentally discouraged from running. What if, in holding athletes accountable to those wrongdoings, we could also solve the fundamental root of the problem that caused the discouraged behavior? To do so, we need to consider where that behavior comes from, and what we *really* want our athletes to learn from the punishment.

So what are our options? Sometimes, the solution is in the presentation of the punishment. For example, in women's lacrosse, players are not allowed to wear any jewelry on the field. If an official notices earrings or a bracelet - even a headband taken out of the hair and wrapped around the risk - a minor foul is assessed, and the team wearing the jewelry loses possession. One of the times I find running appropriate is when anyone still has jewelry on when practice has started. If captains or teammates see it before I do, they remind the athlete, like they would before a game, and we go about our day. But if I see it first, the offenders and the captains run. They don't run because I want to punish them; they run because that's an appropriate consequence. During a game, if no one reminded a teammate to get her jewelry out, we would lose possession, and the whole team would have to run back to our defensive side. When I tell them to run for punishment in that case, I have to communicate it that way. Running is not punishment I am dishing out because I am the coach and I am in charge; it's a reminder of what would happen if you made that mistake in a game. In that way, running addresses the root of the problem. But what about problems that really aren't addressed by running? Far more of those kind of problems, large and small, preventable and inevitable, will come up on any team.

One year, one of my captains, we'll call her Alyssa (not her real name), came into my room during the fall to tell me that she was going on a week-long field trip with the history department over spring break - right in the middle of our season. I had known Alyssa since she was in sixth grade. She was one of the first girls to come through the program after I got involved helping the youth. She was one of the most dedicated, coachable athletes I ever had. I was, at first, shocked that she would make the decision to leave the team in the middle of the season during her senior year, as a captain, no less. Other coaches I talked to suggested that she shouldn't be a captain if she wasn't going to be there for that week. I could not formulate a clear case against that, except that Alyssa was voted captain by her team, and everything she had done since the sixth grade had demonstrated to me and her peers that she was the right girl for the job. Taking away her captainship might have created more problems than it solved. I also had the benefit of time. This was not a heat-of-the-moment decision; my perception was not skewed by the pressure and immediacy of competition. I also held no ill-will for her. I did not want to punish Alyssa to make her feel bad about going on the trip. It was a school-sponsored trip, a once-in-a-lifetime learning experience. She shouldn't have felt bad about wanting to go.

All of that said, a captain going away for a week of the season is a problem. I could not just ignore it. We have a policy, consistent across the athletic program, that you must be present for varsity sports during school breaks. If one of our captains was going to miss a whole week, we had to do something. So I thought about it: what about going on the trip was causing a problem from the athletics standpoint? The answers I came up with were that it gave the impression that she was not committed to the sport or the team. Of course, as I mentioned before, everything she did over the six years I knew her told a different story. The problem was not that she was not committed but that people might perceive her to be uncommitted. The domino effect of that perception could ripple through the program and create a crisis of team culture. No amount of running would fix that.

Before I even had any ideas for her "punishment," I sat down and explained everything in the last two paragraphs. Together with the other captain, we came up with a plan to solve the problem: a "punishment." Alyssa was going to call a team meeting to explain her decision, emphasizing that the team meant the world to her, but she was confident they could get through the week's games without her, and when she weighed the one week of lacrosse against a once-in-a-lifetime opportunity to go abroad, she decided to go on the trip. She was going to take charge of all preseason planning, including organizing practices and offering private lessons to any underclassmen who were looking to improve. We, Alyssa, the other captain, and I, agreed doing those things would be the best she could do to address the real problem: the perception of her lack of commitment. I cannot give a blueprint of "if-then" approaches to problem solving in this way; I can only suggest that your approach to rules and control is about identifying the actual problem that needs to be addressed and addressing it in a way that teaches something more than, "Coach is in charge" and "I hate running."

Chapter 5

It's Not About Fun

Keeping track of wins and championships, team and individual statistics, makes competitive sports a much better learning environment than casual recreational sports. When we harness our competitive drive to measure ourselves against our expectations, our goals, and our opponents, we tap into a great motivator for self-improvement. Unlike learning in a classroom setting, learning on the athletic field is inherently more enjoyable. Playing sports releases endorphins and gives us a sense of community. At a young age, that is enough for kids. They should have fun when they are learning a sport, and it should remain fun to play the game as they get older. But that fun is inherent in the activity, not a product of the structure the coach brings to the competitive level. At higher competitive levels, our job is to harness what makes the sport "fun" to turn it into a great classroom for many skills that don't show up in the high school curriculum. The fruits of that are not just wins, championships, and individual accolades; they are skills and lessons that will bear far greater rewards for our athletes in their adult lives.

It's About Enjoyment

Enjoyment does not mean fun. Fun is fleeting, light, and often relaxing. Enjoyment is much deeper, more significant, and more productive. Once we advance beyond the youth and recreational levels, athletes grow to understand that they can enjoy the discipline and structure that competitive sports have to offer. Laughing and joking around with friends during a water break (or heaven forbid, in line for a drill) is a light-hearted, fleeting form of fun. That kind of fun is an important part of a balanced life, and there is a time and place for it. In the world of competitive sports, that time is after practice, on the bus home from a game, or at team social events. For athletes who are trained to enjoy the work of practice, light-hearted fun is distracting and counter-productive when it happens in the wrong time.

I never played sports at a very high level, but even in little league baseball and JV basketball, I learned to enjoy the time I spent practicing. I was engaged in challenges that coaches set for me, and I learned early to practice deliberately, "gamifying" my practice with little goals or methods of accountability. Every once in a while, I get together with some friends to play pickup basketball. I arrive about an hour early and run myself through shooting drills that I made up. And I love it. I am engaged in the moment, and, as cliché as it sounds, all of my worries, my external pressures, fade away for a little while. For me, that was the most important lessons sports taught. That feeling of being fully engaged in meaningful tasks came up again

"... Our job is to harness what makes the sport "fun" to turn it into ... skills and lessons that will bear far greater rewards for our athletes in their adult lives."

when I was studying for big projects in college, in my current career when I run a practice, and at this moment as I write these words.

Because of sports, I learned to enjoy the process of improving myself. That might be the most important long-term lesson we can teach our athletes. When they move on to their life after sports, they will know not only that challenges can be overcome, but that they can actually enjoy themselves while they work to overcome those challenges. Athletes, who understand that losing yourself completely in challenging work can be fun in that sense, seek out challenges and perform better than their peers because they understand how to enjoy working hard.

It's About Ambition

In preseason goal-setting meetings, underclassmen usually come up with pretty timid goals. They want to make the varsity team or get some playing time in varsity games. They want to set goals they know they can achieve. By my definition, a goal you know you can achieve is an expectation; a goal has to be more ambitious. In fact, sports psychologists suggest that you should set goals that you think you have a 10-40% chance of accomplishing. Anything less is not enough to get excited about. We want to encourage our kids to set ambitious goals and to keep working for them. The girl who should make the varsity roster should make it her goal to earn a starting spot, and the girl who expects to earn a starting spot should make it her goal to be an all-conference player. They won't all reach their goals every year, and we won't always reach our team goals. But that's the point of goal-setting. If you only set goals you can reach, then you'll never know what you could have achieved. We don't set goals; we define our ambitions. Once our athletes are done with sports, they can take that lesson with them in their professional lives. Set ambitious goals and work hard to reach them but don't be too disappointed if you fall short. It's acceptable to miss a goal if that goal is ambitious enough.

In our program, a lot of the individual and partner drills don't change from the youngest level to the high school varsity team. They look incredibly different when performed by a beginner at 8 years old or an All-American in her senior year, but the actual instructions don't change; they just get better at it. In many of those drills, I will tell them, at any level, "If you're not dropping the ball, you're not trying hard enough." In other words, I want them pushing themselves to find their limits because, once they have found how hard they can throw until it's too fast for their partner, they can keep working up to and beyond that point. If they never throw it too hard, then they never actually threw it hard enough.

The same holds true when they are defining their ambitions before a season. When they are done with sports, it's even more important. Playing competitive sports is the only time in life that goals have a very short expiration date. If an athlete decides that having a 50-goal season is her goal, and she doesn't get there, she has failed to meet her goal. But if that was a good, ambitious goal for her, then she has not failed. She probably had a better season than she would have if she made her goal less ambitious. Failing to meet expectations should be disappointing; failing to meet goals is just a part of life.

When the season ends, that goal is no longer attainable, but in almost any other ambition she can have in her life, there will not be such a final expiration date. If you want a promotion, and you don't get it, you can get back to work and apply next time. The same is true for pretty much any goal you can set in your adult life. Failing to reach goals is nothing to be ashamed of. If anything, setting goals that are ambitious enough to fail will take you much farther in life than the more common practice of confusing "goals" with "expectations."

It's About Growth

Growth is structured, deliberate development and observable improvement. All of the other pieces I've discussed contribute to the growth of a person on your team, but growth can also be sport-specific. An athlete seeing improvement and development towards goals is experiencing growth. Perfecting their foul shot or four-foot putting stroke may not help the athlete succeed outside of sports, but the process and recognition of growth can.

Growth goes hand-in-hand with enjoyment, ambition, and engagement. It might be fun to shoot around with your friends at the beach, but that will have a very limited impact on helping you grow. Going to a hoop by yourself and engaging in a step-back shooting drill, however, where you start at the block and move back to the three point line one step at a time on each made shot, is going to lead to much more growth. You have a goal (make all of the shots to keep moving back), and the structure of the drill helps you focus. As the old cliché goes, "Practice doesn't make perfect; perfect practice makes perfect." I would go one step further and say perfect isn't even the goal of practice. The goal of practice is *progress*. The goal is growth.

In my early years coaching, I was way too results-oriented. Focusing too much on results means, by definition, that I did not have room to focus on all these other ideas that lead to successful coaching and team building. During one of our great seasons when I had only coached for a few years, we had a great run going. We had lost just one of our first 12 games and were going to be the one seed in our conference tournament. But the girls were feeling the drag of a long season. To try to break up the monotony, we instituted "Funday Monday," a day once in a while when we could leave the lacrosse sticks and just come out and play. The goal was just to have fun. One day, we played ultimate frisbee. Another day, we broke into two teams and played football, with me and an assistant coach playing opposing quarterbacks. We had fun. It was a break, but looking back, it's not something I'm proud of.

Funday Monday was not a bad idea for what the team needed, but I later realized that it was the results-driven culture of the team that necessitated that day "off." One of our captains unknowingly pointed that out to me when she was talking to a younger girl about what it takes to become a great athlete. "After my sophomore year," she explained, "lacrosse became more of a job." She meant that in a proud, positive way. She meant that she had to commit to working out on her own to get better, to join a premier team, get girls together in the off-season, and fully engage in the sport. In short, she meant that it became a job she wanted to do, but the statement still didn't strike my ear right. I'm not sure I want my athletes thinking of their sport as a job before they are even old enough to drive.

Much later, I realized that the reason it felt like a job was that I treated her like an employee. I had a set of goals that I needed the team to meet, and they worked like crazy to get the job done. I kept practice exciting, productive, and mostly enjoyable, but the focus on result-oriented team goals (wins and championships) wore on them. The focus became pressure. The pressure began to feel like a job. That season was a great example of a time when winning masked a lot of problems. Every win, the pressure grew. The captains unloaded the pressure by being tough on their teammates, organizing mandatory team events, trying to keep control over everyone. But as long as we won, we felt good, and potential problems never reached the surface. We were having a good time and meeting goals, but we still needed those days off to recharge. Funday Monday was a Band-Aid for a stressful, results-oriented team culture. And when we finally lost a big game, that Band-Aid was useless.

Even before the loss in the conference championship game, the tensions were boiling over. Unbeknownst to me, a captain and a future All-American had screamed at each other just before going out for the pre-game warmup. We walked in our tight formation, silent, looking focused and intense. As we walked by, a fan called out, "That's a disciplined team, coach," to compliment me. He thought he saw the determination and focus of a comfortable, well-prepared championship unit. We were actually an over-stressed group of individuals, a little sick of the company of one another, waiting to crack under the increasing pressure. And when we cracked, we crashed. Hard.

Because I had focused so much on the results, losing the championship was thought impossible, unacceptable. Even in practice, I framed all the work and learning in terms of how it would help us win, not how it would help us *grow*. That mentality cost us. Because we learned that we can't always win, some girls decided they didn't want to try anymore. The next season, three varsity contributors decided not to come back for their senior seasons. They were nice about it; they simply told me they wanted to focus on other things as they got ready for college, but I knew, even if they didn't realize it, they quit because they didn't need the stress anymore. While the one captain had thought positively of the team as a *job*, not everyone did. I had sent the message loud and clear by the way I ran the team: "If we're not the best, we might as well not show up." We lost four games that year, including the conference and state championship. Since we weren't the best, several athletes literally did not show up for the following season.

I realized pretty quickly that was what happened, and I worked hard to correct it for the next season. I attended clinics about team building, read some great releases by the Positive Coaching Alliance, and committed myself to focusing on process instead of results. In other words, everything I said and did with the athletes was going to emphasize growth, slow, steady, deliberate growth for each individual and the team as a whole. We would play to our own standard, not our opponents, and I would respond to our performance relative to our potential, not our record. But the damage was done. It took until every girl who lost those two championship games had graduated to feel that I had succeeded in developing a growth-focused culture.

I knew we had transformed the culture on one Funday Monday. We were 9-0, about to head into our toughest game of the season. Every practice, I emphasized each girl getting a little better at something. Every drill ran great, every practice felt productive and energetic. Cries of, "Wow, practice is already over?" rang out every day. Girls wanted to work hard because they knew they were growing. They could see it in their individual performances and the team's success on game days. So, at 9-0, with our toughest game of the year coming up, I came to practice without the balls, a big smile, and said, "Today is Funday Monday. Leave your stuff in your bags!" For the first time in my career, I was met with . . . disappointment. The girls who were already up and using equipment rushed to get a few more catches in or finish the pile of balls to shoot. The captains came to me and asked, "Do we have to do a fun day?" They wanted another grueling practice of fast drills, conditioning, and lots of competition because they knew it helped them *grow*. They didn't care if it helped them win, or, if they did, they understood winning was a byproduct of growing, and they didn't want to miss out on another day of it.

This is perhaps the most important lesson I have for any coach. Shifting from a focus on winning to a focus on growth will have an immediate impact on the culture of a team, the quality of practices, and eventually, in the long-term, results on the field. But it is also an important shift for the long-term well-being of our athletes. They will very rarely be in a one-chance, win-or-lose situation when they are no longer playing sports. By focusing on growth instead of results (or the opposite: lighthearted fun), we are teaching our athletes to enjoy the work that goes into growing. We are teaching them the importance of studying, reading on their own, reflecting on their experiences. Athletes can grow in myriad ways after their playing careers are over, so emphasizing growth is one of the most important actions a coach can take for the long-term impact on our athletes.

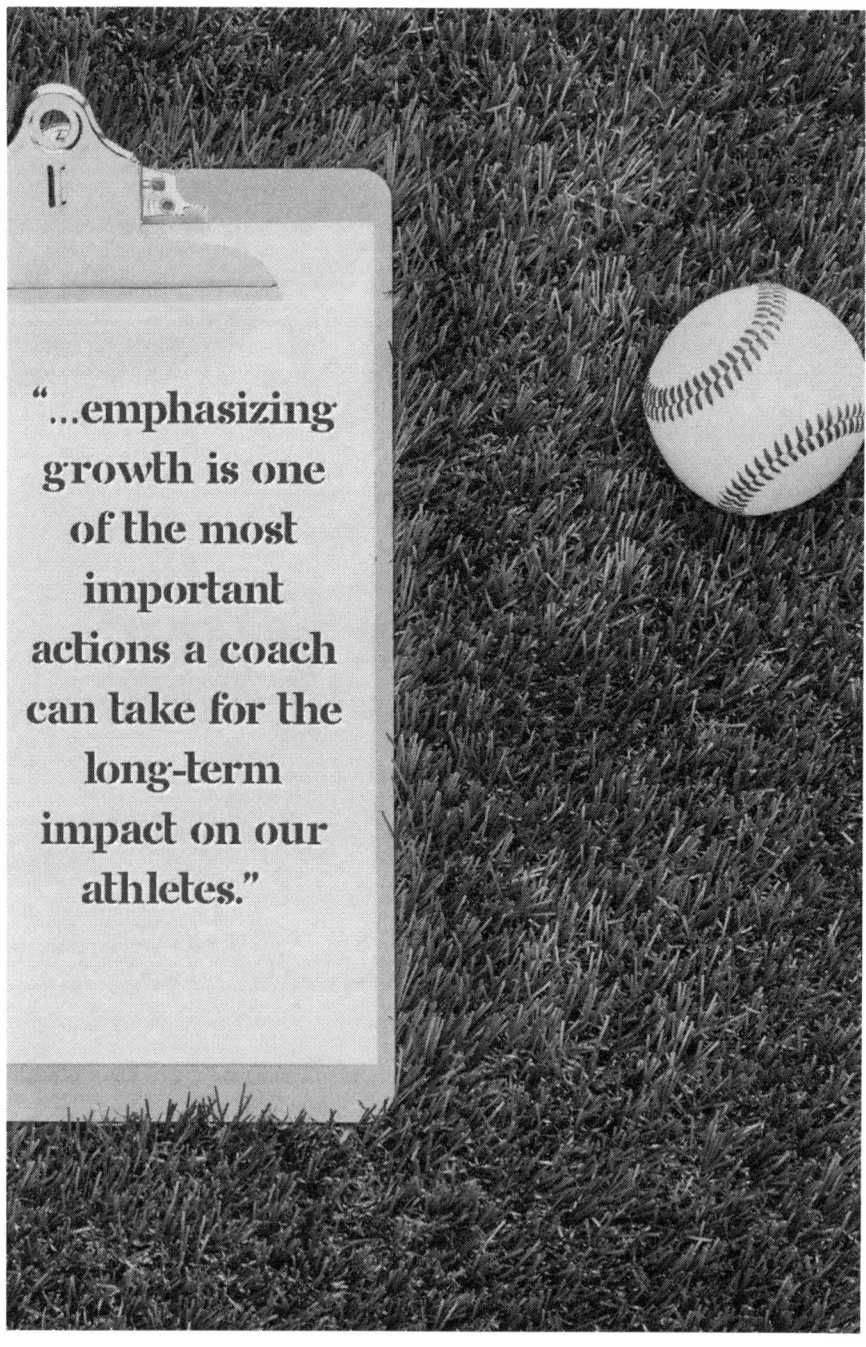

"...emphasizing growth is one of the most important actions a coach can take for the long-term impact on our athletes."

Conclusion:

It's Not About You

You should work hard to be the best coach you can be, and you can be a very important influence in the lives of young people. It's important to remember that work doesn't get much attention from people outside your organization. Doing that work well will get you high fives, thank you notes, and hugs, but it won't get you headlines. If the coach is getting a lot of attention, that's probably not a good thing. While you are important in the lives of the young people you guide, you are not *that* important to the success of the team. Don't let your ego tell you otherwise.

A coach should be focused on leaving a legacy in the hearts and minds of their athletes - not leaving a display case of trophies and a stack of headlines. Bad things happen quickly; good things take time. No matter what level you coach, you won't get public praise for doing the slow, good work of coaching. You might get attention for winning at the high school, college, or professional level, but that is fleeting. Losing happens fast, and the attention turns negative. When you focus on your athletes, develop relationships, and create a great team environment, you might get headlines and trophies, but that won't define you, so the loss of them in any given season won't define you either.

"A coach should be focused on leaving a legacy in the hearts and minds of their athletes..."

That's why our focus should be on developing relationships and teaching the sport and the life lessons that come along with it. If I had to choose, I'd rather have a phone call when a former athlete gets a new job or a thank you note when they graduate than a bunch of trophies on the shelves. I do believe you can accomplish both, but always remember that will have more to do with the athletes on your team than with your coaching. The coach's job is to love, support, and nurture their athletes. To pay attention to each one, to push them to be their best, and create an environment in which they feel safe with their team, excited about their sport, successful on the field, and set up for success after sports.

When he got his first head coaching job, my father posted a poem in his office, "Indispensable Man" by Saxon White Kessinger. The poem advises anyone who thinks they are important to fill a bucket with water and splash around for a while then take their hand out and wait a minute. The bucket will be exactly as it was before. "The moral of this quaint example," the final stanza explains:

"Is do just the best that you can,

Be proud of yourself but remember,

There's no indispensable man." [2]

And If you ever find yourself feeling too important, remember this: the first year Bill Belichick and Tom Brady were on separate teams, Brady won the Superbowl, and Belichick's team didn't make the playoffs.

Thanks and Acknowledgements

To every athlete I've coached, every coach I've worked alongside, every administrator I've driven crazy, and everyone who has challenged, inspired, and taught me along the way—this book exists because of you. Coaching is a privilege, and I am forever grateful for the lessons, the memories, and the countless moments that have shaped me.

And especially thanks for Shawn Gavin and Jill Temple, who put up with my 5am texts, planning for contingencies that will never happen, and picking up the stuff I've left strewn about the field after practice. And somehow keep agreeing to come back and do it all again, year after year.

About the Author

I grew up in a college football locker room, soaking everything in while my Dad built competitive, championship programs at multiple levels. When I wasn't in the locker room, I was with my four female cousins and two sisters - all of whom played competitive sports, and are currently instilling competitive athleticism into a new generation. So, I guess it's natural that I ended up becoming a coach of women's sports.

Before I made the leap to be a full-time college coach, I spent a decade teaching English and coaching multiple sports at my alma mater, Daniel Hand High School, in Madison, CT. I like to think the background in English is not the only thing I have in common with John Wooden, but he had a lot more hardware that I currently do. The best thing about coaching is that I always feel like I'm just getting started. When I'm done with a season I immediately look forward to the next one - another chance to achieve. Like riding off into the sunrise.

End Notes

1. Will, Brian. <u>The Dropout Millionaire: 37 Business Lessons on How to Succeed with no money, no education, and no clue.</u> Bookmark Publishing House. 2021.

2. White Kessinger, Saxon. *"Indispensable Man." appleseeds.org,* 23 April 2025. https://www.appleseeds.org/indispen-man_saxon.htm

Photography and Image Source

Back Cover headshot photograph of the author-photography credited to Southern Connecticut State University Athletics and Recreation.